Perhaps the earliest photograph of Cromer beach, c.1850

Foreword

It is now over 210 years since Edmund Bartell wrote his guide to Cromer and began the written record. Since then we have had Mrs Sargant's *Guide to Cromer by a Visitor*, the scholarly research by Walter Rye, the detailed compilation brought together by Alfred Savin, the booklet published by Cyril Crawford Holden and Christopher Pipe's 'Dictionary of Cromer and Overstrand History'.

When Cromer Museum opened in 1976, Martin Warren became its first permanent curator. He served in that office for over 20 years before taking on a wider responsibility within the Norfolk Museums Service. Fortunately he has brought together his wide knowledge of the history of Cromer together on a number of occasions for publication. This short history was first published in 1988 and has already gone through three editions. For the fourth time it is republished, with amendments and additions by Poppyland Publishing. As we seek to maintain the balance between what we value from the past and the demands of the present and future, such a booklet as this is a valuable starting point for our thoughts.

It would also be appropriate to remind local readers that the Museum is always happy to receive new material. Much of the initial collection is from the Victorian and Edwardian period, when Cromer was widely photographed. It is now time to ensure that important photographs and documentation from between the wars and into the 1950s and 1960s are offered to the Museum. They will receive a safe home there, where they can be conserved for future interest.

The lost village of Shipden

The lobster retreats deep into its stony hold as two divers descend to the bed of the green North Sea, 400 metres from the Bath House Hotel on the promenade at Cromer. When they reach the bottom and their eyes became accustomed to the gloom they see it. Stark and forbidding, the pile of stones stands like a tombstone for a forgotten village. A circular stump of flint cobbles set in mortar, almost two metres high and more than that across. This is the biggest piece remaining of what the fishermen have known for centuries as the Church Rock. By popular belief these are the remains of the church of St Peter which served the village of Shipden in the Middle Ages. But like the rest of the settlement the church was undermined as the sea sapped the base of the cliff. Now nothing remains of the old village except these stones and a few other slabs of wall nearby on the seabed. The timbers and thatch of old Shipden have left no trace. The majority of the stones of the flint buildings lie anonymously on the seabed. They are thick with marine growth and provide homes for crabs. At low spring tides the Church Rock and other ruins to the west of the pier were once visible.

Church Rock lay untouched except for the battering of the waves and the occasional touch of an oar from a passing crab boat. Until that is 8th August 1888, when the paddle steamer *Victoria* set off from Cromer bound for Yarmouth. To the horror of the onlooking fishermen she hit the rock and stuck fast. All her passengers were taken off and they returned to Yarmouth by train. Attempts were made to salvage her by a tug and two lighters but the ropes parted and she became a total wreck. A steam traction engine was brought to the Gangway in the hope of hauling some of the wreckage ashore but the distance was too great and the engine could not even pull the slack out of the hawser. Eventually Trinity House blew up the wreck and Church Rock was damaged. Consequently it is no longer seen. As A. C. Savin quipped, in his history of Cromer, this is probably the only

The rural fishing village of Cromer clustered around its decaying medieval church, depicted in a print published in 1779

known instance of a ship being wrecked on a portion of a church.

There is little of Shipden for the archaeologist to investigate and the historian is almost equally unlucky. Documentary evidence is meagre, no map exists, and there are few details at all beyond the clerk's ancient records such as who held which manor and what taxes were paid. We might assume that it stood much as Cromer does today in an amphitheatre, nestling between the higher ground and the sea. At a low point in the cliffs a small stream draining to the sea had cut a deep cleft in the sand and clay. We know this cleft today as the Gangway. Twenty miles westwards the saltmarsh ports of Cley, Blakeney and Wiveton grew wealthy on their trade. To the east there was no place for a ship to anchor until Yarmouth was reached. The site at Shipden was an obvious one to choose for a settlement on this bleak and harbourless coast, offering a natural gangway to the beach and a place to pull up boats out of the reach of the tide. As well as farming, with barley and sheep, what wealth Shipden enjoyed must have been founded on trade and fishing. Some earlier authors have supposed that there was low ground beside the sea, with a proper harbour, but on geological grounds this suggestion is unlikely. There was probably envy of the natural harbours to the west for at Cromer there was only an open beach. But the merchants of Shipden managed to carry on their trade none the less.

In William the Conquerer's Domesday Survey there is no mention at all of Cromer; only manors in the parish of Shipden (spelt in various ways: 'Shipedana', 'Shipden', 'Sceptre' and 'Scipedana'). The historian Walter Rye, thinking of its importance as a port, wondered if it was derived from 'Ship-hill', but perhaps the 'ship' really meant 'sheep' that grazed on the grassy hills of the Cromer ridge. In time, as erosion proceeded, Shipden came to be known as Cromer. The two are linked in numerous medieval and later documents in the form of 'Cromer alias Shipden' and vice versa. Rye also states, with some plausibility, that many of the local place names, including Cromer, can be traced to Danish places and were the result of the settlement by the Danes.

Near the gap in the cliffs leading down to the beach was a wooden pier. Above it on the cliff was a cluster of buildings around the parish churches of Shipden-juxta-Mare and Shipden-juxta-Felbrigg. Most likely it was the remains of the former, dedicated to St Peter, that went over the cliff some time in the fourteenth century and that now lie on the seabed off Cromer. On the site of the other, St Paul's, the present church was built. It is dedicated to St Peter and St Paul and is more than large enough to hold the two congregations.

The merchants and fishermen

Amongst the earliest records mentioning the town, the merchants feature prominently along with the fishermen. Evidently trade was important to the economy and doubtless Shipden owed much of its prosperity to trade. In 1285 the king granted a Friday market and a yearly feast of eight days. These brought a valuable income to the Lord of the Manor. At fairs almost anything might occur but the principal activity was buying and selling. Villagers could obtain wares not normally available to them.

In 1333 the richest merchants paid their taxes: Alan fil' Galfridi paid 6 shillings, Isabel Tebald 3s (she also paid 20s in Northrepps), Clement Hervey 3s, Robert Mosse 2s 6d, John Waryn 2s 6d, Alan Reymund 2s 2d, William Smith 2s, William Leman 2s and 27 others paid lesser sums. Evidently the inroads of the sea were not unduly affecting the prosperity at this time. In the mid-fourteenth century manufacturing and commerce in England were affluent and expanding. The king prohibited the export of corn from Cromer in 1350, except that is for shipment to Calais. This had been recently captured by the English in their struggle for the French crown. One wonders whether any notice was taken of the order.

By a list of dues to be paid in order to finance the first known pier we have an inkling of the kind of trade Cromer enjoyed. In 1391 the King granted licence for the men of Shipden to levy duties on merchandise passing through the port, for five years.

For every last of herring exposed for sale	2d
For vaga (an eighth or bag of salt)	2d
For hundred of rygolds (deal planks)	3d
For hundred of wainscot (oak)	1d
For hundred tunholt	½d
For barrel of pitch or turpentine	½d
For barrel of oil	2d
For every hundred of fir spars	1d
For every thousand of dascell	1d
For every thousand of iron	4d
For every quarter of corn and malt, of whatever sort	½d
For every chaldron of seacoal	1d
For every hundred of fish, called 'Orgoys', reckoned by ten score	12d
For every lob, ling and cod	6d
For every boat laden with articles for sale	1d
For every horse laden with articles for sale	½d
For every ship putting in with merchandise within the aforesaid	4d
For every boat called 'fissher' laden with merchandise	1d
For every other saleable article not mentioned above coming to the said town and market of the value of five shillings, except wool, leather, fleeces, lead, tin and wine	¼d

In 1565 a survey of the ports, creeks and landing places of Norfolk tells us that

> this town hathe a landinge place called the peere and ther be housholders in the same towne to the number of 117 and the saide landing place is in the governannce of the Quenes Majestie and by the auctoritie of the customer controller and Sercher of the porte of Yarmouth Shippes are comonlye licensed to ladd and unladd ther.
>
>> Mariners and ffishermen inhabitinge in
>> this Towne to the nomber of: 48

There were 117 householders in Cromer at this time but for some reason this document records no trading vessels.

There was a constant sea traffic between Norfolk and the northeast of England for coal. But other commodities came from much further away. Although the ships were small they managed to range over most of the North Sea, into the Baltic and even to Iceland and Greenland.

The coal and corn trade

Needs of the district that could not be satisfied locally were imported and were probably expensive. For heavy goods this could only be achieved by sea and there was a steady traffic of vessels plying the waters of the east coast. From at least the year 1391 until railways stole the trade, coal was brought to Cromer and surrounding districts from Sunderland by colliers which came onto the beach. The exports of the area, principally wheat, barley and malt, also left by sea. It seems strange now that sizeable vessels were able to trade at Cromer but for centuries this was practically the only type of trade there was. At high water the wooden ships carrying about 90 to 120 tons came to the shore, until they touched the sandy beach. They waited for the tide to drop then horses and carts came down from the town to collect the cargo. Coal was unloaded via wooden chutes and when the carts were full an extra horse or mule was hitched on to haul it up the steep gangway. The Gangway was just a sandy roadway until 1882, in 1901 it was paved with granite setts. These were laid at an angle to provide a grip for the horses' hooves. Two rows of long smooth stones were for cartwheels to run on. When the collier ships were empty sand was loaded as ballast and on the rising tide they floated off. They were

The Gangway in 1875

A rare occasion in 1867 or shortly after when three coal ships – the Wensleydale, *the* Commerce *and the* Ellis *(or* Plumper*) – were beached together at the bottom of the Gangway. The ravine was later filled in and the beck was channelled through a pipe under the new promenade. Today's Gangway is off the left of the photograph.*

assisted by a hawser connected to anchors fixed in the rocks off shore.

A directory of 1792 names the eight vessels belonging to Cromer together with the merchants who owned them. But by the 1860s there were only three vessels – the *Wensleydale*, the *Commerce* and the *Ellis*. They continued to trade until they could no longer compete with the cheaper and less hazardous railway. The *Ellis* made her final voyage in 1887 and so ended a trade which had continued for centuries.

Piers and sea defences

The early piers and jetties probably served a dual purpose, assisting perhaps with the loading and unloading of trading and fishing vessels and providing safety. But principally they acted as a groyne to help protect the cliffs. The exposed position meant it was difficult and expensive to provide safe harbourage and the building of piers taxed the resources of the local community to the utmost. The first known mention of a pier comes in 1391 in letters patent granting the right to levy the duties listed above. From the mid-fifteenth century onwards scarely a man died without leaving money in his will to maintain it.

The pier took a hammering during storms. In 1483 40 shillings was left for great stones to be placed opposite the pier, perhaps as a sort of sea wall. About a century later a dispute occurred over monies received for the reparation of a wall which might have been a sea wall. By 1551 the inhabitants were complaining to King Henry VIII's Counsel that a great many houses had been swallowed up by the sea, despite the 'great piers' that had been erected at great cost as a defence. Added to this there had lately been a fire which had consumed a whole street of thatched houses. In consideration of this and other matters they requested relief from the normal burden of taxes. Shortly before 1580 a further attempt was made to erect a pier, but it proved to be futile. Then in 1582 Queen Elizabeth granted the right the inhabitants to export wheat, barley and malt for the maintenance of their town and towards the (re)building of an 'ould decayed peere there'.

Little more is heard of Cromer pier until the eighteenth century when an attempt was made to revive the flagging trade. An ambitious project was begun to erect a pier or harbour financed by subscription and duties levied on goods. A start was made in 1731 but in September of the following year the project may well have foundered. A local clergyman, Patrick St Clair, recorded that the sea had deposited 'a heap of stones and sand almost as big as [his] house into the bason and fill'd up quite the north west passage, so that many people gave the project over for lost; but they have begun to sett down their timbers, and have removede all the stones that lay in their way to the laying down their frames of wood, and I hope they will secure it for this winter'.

On the shore at the present day, to the east of the pier groyne, if the beach is very low, one can see two rows of wooden piles extending out from the shore and turning to the east run off at an angle. The westward side appears to have been close-boarded. It might be the remains of one of the earlier jetties, but which one it is hard to say. It would appear to be designed to give shelter to vessels, while the close boarding would also act as a groyne.

An old jetty was there in 1816 and was illustrated by William Collins. When Robert Dixon drew it in 1820 it was very decayed. A new one was erected in 1822, using cast iron supports from William Hase's foundry at Saxthorpe, but this was damaged in 1836 and finally destroyed in 1845. The last of the wooden jetties was put up in 1846 at the time of the building of a flint seawall. It was a plain wooden structure just 70 yards long but it provided the focus for Victorian gentlefolk who promenaded its boards by day and by night and its use was regulated by several by-laws. Smoking was only allowed after nine o'clock when all ladies would be expected to have retired for the evening. Common folk and servants in livery were disdained and on Sundays the visitors withdrew to allow the inhabitants of Cromer free liberty of their own jetty. Briefly, in the early 1890s, the jetty had been embellished with a band stand on stilts at the promenade end but for the most part it was a sombre retreat for gentlefolk who wished to stroll or sit a while on its wooden bench. Damage was sustained in 1890, probably by a vessel striking it, and the last few legs were replaced by cast iron ones. In December 1897 it was doomed when it was struck again and further damaged by gales, so that it had to be dismantled and the materials sold off by auction. For a brief spell the beach was devoid of pier or jetty and it seemed naked. Earlier plans for a screw-pile pier had come to nothing but the loss of the jetty spurred the Protection Commissioners on. They commissioned a pier that would spear-head the fashionable and growing resort into the twentieth century.

Cromer's present pier is something of a crowning glory and provides a glorious seaward prospect of the town. Sadly the wonderful cast iron gates between cupola-topped kiosks and the ornate gaslights were swept away in post-war zeal.

The new pier, shortly after it opened in 1901. Admission 2d, and 6d to enter the bandstand enclosure where the Blue Viennese Band were playing.

But the Edwardian Pavilion Theatre roof remains. The annual summer show proudly claims to be the last remaining genuine 'end of the pier show', where veteran stars and young hopefuls team up in a modern version of the Victorian music hall. Below decks, the fragile and corroding structure must be constantly maintained against the battering of the salt sea. Since it was built in 1900 the pier has never made a penny profit, but preserving this relic is vital if Cromer is to remain a proper seaside resort. Piers are an endangered species and Cromer is like a natural habitat. This pleasure pier is but the latest and grandest of the long line of piers and jetties. Let us hope it will be giving pleasure for many years to come. It is unlikely we shall get another if we lose it.

The new and old lighthouses, from a print by J. B. Ladbrooke. The old lighthouse fell in 1866.

Lighthouses

The earliest light for mariners was a fire burning on a platform half way up the church tower. The platform is still there today on the north-west corner, built into the angle between two buttresses; the light is commemorated in the church's modern stained glass.

The elegant lighthouse was built in 1833

In 1717 a brick lighthouse was erected on the hills to the east of the town. It was at first also illuminated by coal fires and later on it was powered by 15 patent oil lamps with three-foot reflectors. The light was rotated by clockwork machinery and the whole lighthouse was tended by two ladies who reputedly kept the place very neat and tidy.

The sea's advance continued and when in 1832 a particularly big cliff fall threatened the lighthouse another was built further inland. This is the one that stands there today, little altered but for the addition of a modern lamp house. The old one stood an empty shell until it finally fell over the cliff in 1866.

The East Cliff from the jetty in 1809. On the left are fortifications to protect the Gangway and boathouses at beach level. Note the runway up to Ditchell's Barn on the right, used to carry up merchandise.

The threat of invasion

The people on the Norfolk coast have lived in constant fear of invasion from the sea. In 1588 at the time of the Spanish Armada a chain of beacons was established around the coast of Britain. One of these was on the Beacon Hill at Trimingham and another was at Roman Camp, West Runton. From Weybourne to Cley extra defences were built to counter the threat. When John Taylor the poet and London waterman made a forced landing at Cromer the ship and its crew were spied by some women and children who gave the alarm that pirates or invaders were coming; an armed gang of townsfolk came and took them prisoner. His poem published in 1623 records the incident and gives an idea of what a lusty band of adventurers the locals were at that time, ready to take to arms or to their boats to capture enemies or seek rewards.

At the end of the eighteenth century there was widespread fear that the French would invade. An incident in 1797 goaded local action. A ship came inshore apparently in need of a pilot and local boatmen went out to offer assistance. However, as they approached, a swivel gun was pointed at them and they were warned off. A brave boy aboard the ship shouted out that she had been captured by the French and so the Cromer men quickly came ashore and armed themselves with muskets. They gave chase in two fishing smacks and eight hours later they succeeded in capturing the ship and her crew of seven French and one American. One contemporary account says that the ship was taken to Blakeney, but Thomas Fowell Buxton (parliamentarian, anti-slavery worker and member of the local gentry) recorded in his notebook that he had been told of the incident by his parents when he was a child. Their belief was that the ship was a French privateer and that it had been brought to Cromer and placed at the bottom of the Gangway. There it was filled with stones and concrete and used as a protection. The remnants of just such a boat-shaped structure of wood and stone were still there when early photographs recorded the Gangway in the 1870s. At the top of the Gangway is a row of old coastguard cottages, converted from a granary. Beside the garden wall is a cannon set up as a post and it was alleged that this also came out of the 'privateer'.

Early nineteenth-century drawings show a fortification on the cliff at the top of the Gangway and also guns trained seawards at the end of Jetty Street. In 1797 a meeting of local gentlemen and farmers agreed to form a militia called the Cromer Loyal Association and begged the authorities that if they could be supplied with arms and ammunition they would provide their own uniform and serve without pay. Letters pertaining to this and also returns listing their armaments have survived. They had muskets, swords and bayonets but the muskets were poor and rather old and the supply of ammunition was inadequate or slow arriving. Perhaps it is best that Napoleon did not put them to the test.

Bathing and the Georgian resort

Until the eighteenth century it was very popular amongst the well-to-do to indulge in health cures. This was as much a pastime and a social occasion as a cure. It involved drinking mineral spring waters and even bathing in them at inland spas. Bathing in the sea only increased in popularity when Dr Richard Russell recommended its health-giving properties and set up his practice at Brighton. With royal approval sea-bathing caught on and by 1792 the *Universal British Directory* was saying that 'Cromer has for some years past been a summer resort of much genteel company, on account, as well of the beauty and pleasantness of the country about it as of the salubrity of the air and the convenience of the place for bathing'.

It was quite common – especially for men – to bathe in the nude or at best in make-shift costume. But for undressing and getting into the water with due modesty, bathing machines were provided. In 1779 Messrs Terry and Pearson advertised their bathing machine, 'entirely upon a new construction by which bathers are conveyed into and out of the water with Ease, Safety and Expedition'. Dr Sidney Terry was a surgeon who practised in Cromer for more than 30 years until his death in 1796. He was responsible for the construction of private steps from his home in Cliff House (a smaller place then) down to the beach and though there is now a zigzag incline, it is still known as 'Doctor's Steps'.

In 1793 John Gurney of Earlham Hall (now the University of East Anglia) came to Cromer on holiday with his ten children. They stayed in a house opposite

Bathing machines lined up on the beach just to the west of the Gangway

the church, which is now Lloyds pharmacy. His sister Rachel had married Rev Robert Barclay and they had purchased nearby Northrepps Hall in 1790 and lived there with their 12 children. So brother and sister and her husband used to line up their 22 children on the beach and inspect them just for fun. Many of the Gurney children were destined to be influential. There was Elizabeth, later to be Elizabeth Fry of prison reform fame; Hannah, who would marry Thomas Fowell Buxton, MP, who worked with William Wilberforce to bring about the abolition of slavery. They both lived and died in Northrepps Hall. Louisa would marry the third Samuel Hoare and live at Cliff House in Overstrand Road. Then there was Joseph John who with Elizabeth was an active evangelist; and finally Samuel and Daniel, both to attain fame in the banking world.

In the same year that John Gurney moved here Bartlett Gurney built the pretty Northrepps Cottage and two years later John Gurney's brother Joseph purchased a large house on Overstrand Road which he named The Grove. Interrelated with the Gurneys and the Barclays were the Buxtons and the Hoares, who having already spent their holidays here in lodgings, decided to either to buy or build a holiday home at Cromer for the season. So it was within the space of a short time that this great cousinhood of families was established among the local gentry.

Edmund Bartell's account of *Cromer Considered as a Watering Place* in 1800 describes the town for gentlefolk who might consider visiting in search of the picturesque and a little relaxation. He laments that while lodgings may be had for longer visits at three to five guineas a week, there was at that time no large and well-conducted inn. He wondered if an inn would succeed at all as the trade was chiefly confined to the summer, but he need not have worried. George Cooke Tucker was to put that right. He had come to Cromer around 1780, as a tide waiter or collector of dues from ships. He rebuilt the New Inn (or 'Tucker's Hotel' as it was later called) and it stood until the 1960s in the street that still bears his name. It was a well known hotel in its day and coaches left daily for Norwich. Today de Vere Court occupies the site and echoes the Georgian style of Tucker's and also the arcading of the Metropole, a late Victorian hotel that stood beside it.

In 1807 a correspondent to *Bell's Court and Fashionable Magazine* under the pen-name 'Viator' gives a colourful if sneering view of Cromer. He complained that the town had suffered a metamorphosis almost within his own recollection.

> The accommodation for company in this place is of a very humble kind; a few old houses have been taken down and rebuilt within these dozen years, after a more modern and enlarged plan. Some of the fishermen have been ejected from their old cotts, or have surrendered them to a speculating brick-layer, who has spruced them up with a little fresh lath and plaster, or a layer or two of sea-stone and pebbles, and scrawled 'Lodgings to Let' over the window. A chandler and a jobbing carpenter have occasionally leagued together to furnish a room looking towards the sea, with a few chairs, a table and a sopha; a few ale-houses, which not many years ago found it difficult from the penury of the trade, to obtain a licence or a livelihood, are now shot up into hotels or taverns; and a master of a fishing boat, a retailer of crabs has now become the proprietor of a bathing machine.

Quite a number of the buildings of Cromer, for instance in New Street and Chapel Street, date from this period.

Many of the cliff-top sites were redeveloped in the late eighteenth and early nineteenth centuries. Above the Bath Hotel stands Hastings House, once the property of Sir Jacob Astley,

East Promenade photographed in 1857. The Bath House (centre) was turned into a hotel in 1869. Above it Hastings House with the bow window dates from the late eighteenth century.

Lord Hastings, of Melton Constable Hall. It has a magnificent bow window overlooking the beach. Lord Suffield, another of the county gentry, erected his Marine Villa as a summer residence on the prime cliff-top site overlooking the jetty. Shortly before 1823 the Crescent was built and though the roof-lines have been raised and altered this feature still does much to enhance the East Cliff. Brunswick House overlooking the Gangway is a fine example of early nineteenth century taste and quite unaltered.

The correspondent Viator penned his thoughts on the company that thronged to Cromer in those early days.

> The class of person which generally frequents Cromer with few exceptions, is not of the highest order . . . It is here that the Norwich manufacturer who has made his fortune during the last war, takes up his summer retreat and exhibits all the pride and petulance of the counting-house, with the insolence of new-gotten wealth . . . The next class of company . . . are the landed gentlemen of the county and neighbouring provinces . . . They mingle with none but themselves; a man must have a sufficient attestation of his acres and his woods to obtain, if it were worth having, an introduction to them. They repel all advances with a chill and jealous reserve peculiar to themselves.

There was also the incognito society who conspired to keep up a masquerade of wealth and respectability.

Evidently, Cromer was waking up to the commercial possibilities of the seaside resort once the war with France was over and early years of the nineteenth century saw the population expand from 676 in 1801 to 1232 in 1836. There were nine or ten bathing machines on the beach and it could boast of being among the most fashionable sea-bathing places in the kingdom. For 'public entertainment' there were the Tucker's Family Hotel, the Wellington Inn and the Red Lion Inn and on the cliff there was a subscription room where there were daily newspapers, periodicals and a small library for light readers. In addition there were seventy lodgings and boarding houses. The largest of these was Lord Suffield's Marine Villa which had been turned into the Hotel de Paris under the management of Pierre le Francois.

By East Anglian standards the cliffs of the North Norfolk coast are high and rugged and are captivating to those with an eye for the picturesque. Just inland the wooded and heathy hills can trick the eye and in some lights take on the majesty and grandeur of distant mountains. Add to this the animated scenes of industry on the beach as fishermen tended their boats and colliers unloaded and one can see why Cromer became a favourite haunt of artists. A little sketching, perhaps aided by the camera lucida, was just the sort of genteel pastime for the company.

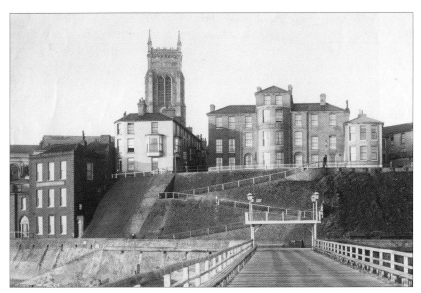

The original Hotel de Paris in 1891, shortly before enlargement. On the left the Lower Tucker's Hotel where the Empress Elizabeth of Austria stayed in 1887.

Renowned artists of the Norwich School such as Robert Dixon, Joseph Stannard, John Sell Cotman, Henry Bright and others all came to North Norfolk, and to Cromer especially, in search of the picturesque.

In the early years of the nineteenth century there were no public card assemblies or ballrooms and so the principal pastimes were walking and riding, either on the beach or through the surrounding countryside. Mary Leak's circulating library was at 38 Church Street, now a jeweller's, and on stilts above the beach was Thomas Randell's bath house. These were resorted to between walks and jaunts with the sketch book. The jetty was a favourite haunt at high water, forming a delightful promenade and occasionally the scene was enlivened by a band to which voluntary donations were made. At low water the expanse of sand in either direction was splendid for walking or riding and on occasions even carriages were driven there.

By 1830 it was said that Cromer had been 'much improved these last years, and the inhabitants, in order to afford their visitors every amusement in their power have established regattas, balls and other entertainments, which are frequented by great numbers – more especially the regattas, when the beach presents a lively and animated scene'.

In the closing years of the eighteenth century there were no traders in the town catering especially for visitors, although there were eight lodging proprietors listed in the directory. By 1832 however there were several who specialised in curiosities and entertainment for the better class of visitor. William Fox was a lapidary and Richard Ransom an amber and jet cutter. In 1836 Ann Fox is listed as a fossil dealer on the Cliff. There was the circulating library and fancy stationers in Church Street, Sarah and Mary Pank had a fancy repository (1845) and Robert Plumbly was a horse and gig lender (1836). Things were slowly waking up.

Early-mid-Victorian resort

The storms of 1836 and 1845 may have caused a great deal of damage but they certainly jolted the town into action, bringing change and improvement to the benefit of the growing resort. By Act of Parliament a sea wall was erected to protect the cliff, extending from the Gangway west to the Melbourne slope. The old jetty of 1822, damaged in 1836 and finally washed away in 1845, was replaced. The first stone of the wall was laid by the Vicar, Rev W. Sharpe, on 21st April 1846, witnessed by the Earl and Countess of Caenarvon and Lord Porchester, which symbolised the quality of people the town was seeking to attract. On the same day the first pile of the new jetty was driven. The works were opened amid much festivity on 7th August. The attractive and sturdy flint wall had a narrow promenade, which was indeed a great asset.

As the prosperity of the resort increased it was clearly worthy of investment. Development went ahead with the building of new hotels and boarding establishments, mostly on the cliff-top and sea front. In 1851 the Belle Vue Hotel was erected to the west side of the Hotel de Paris and next door again was the West

The West beach c.1892, with the Melbourne Hotel at the top of the slope

The Norwich to Cromer coach, from a print engraved by James Pollard, 1830

Cliff Hotel. In 1875 the Lower Tucker's Hotel went up on the Esplanade, connected by a tunnel to the older part of the hotel on top of the cliff. Many other properties belong to this period: Edinburgh House on the East Cliff (1867), the east wing of the Bath Hotel (1872), Kandahar, Western House and the Melbourne Hotel. By mid-Victorian times the frontage of Cromer had almost taken on its modern appearance but the biggest boost to the town's development was to come after the arrival of the railway in 1877.

By the turn of the century the transformation was complete. In many people's opinion it was the most attractive sea front on the east coast. Today it is an agreeable cascade of pantiled roofs virtually hanging over the promenade.

Coaching

Cromer was a relatively important place even in the eighteenth century and coaches plied the routes from Norwich and elsewhere. T. Sanderson was running a coach called the *Diligence* from his hotel in Cromer in 1792 and was so encouraged that he advertised that he would be fitting up another the next year. There would be no more coaches that season however (3rd November) on account of the badness of the roads. There was the mail or post coach, and several other private ones. A blunderbuss used on the Norwich to Cromer Mail Coach is in the museum. There was a more or less daily service between Cromer and Norwich, and several carriers too. The journey took two and a half hours with changes of horses at Roughton, Aylsham and Newton St Faiths.

In 1830 a coach left from the New Inn every Monday, Tuesday and Thursday morning at 8am and every Saturday at 7am, going through Southrepps, North Walsham and Coltishall. From Norwich several carriers went to Cromer daily, as did a post coach from the Angel every afternoon except Sunday. Even in winter the service was only reduced to four days a week.

Cromer was still only accessible by coach (two coaches daily, except Sunday) in 1854. The *Ocean* left from Tucker's Inn and the *Star* from the Belle Vue (now incorporated in the Hotel de Paris). It must have been a long and tiresome journey but Cromer's isolation was solace to genteel and retiring folk who shunned the busier resorts such as Yarmouth. They preferred Cromer's quaint charm, but 'progress' eventually caught up with it.

Railways

The railway reached Cromer relatively late and until then the only way to get there (other than by sea) was by coach. This of course limited the number of visitors who would care to come on account of both the expense and the inconvenience of the journey. The prospectus of 1872 for the building of a railway pointed out the salubrity of Cromer and the beauty of the scenery. Together with its fine beach and sands, it said, this made it a most desirable and attractive watering place. It pointed to the traffic that would be generated by the rich agriculture of the district and that Lord Suffield had released considerable land for housing development. All of this was bound to ensure the success of a railway enterprise. The East Norfolk Railway pushed out from Norwich to North Walsham, completing the line in 1874, and extended to Cromer, opening in March 1877. Thus Cromer was connected with the Great Eastern's main lines to London Liverpool Street. At first the line reached only to the top of the Norwich Road. On the outskirts of town the new Cromer station – later Cromer High – served the newly begun Suffield Park better than it did the holiday trade and the beach. There was a flourishing taxi trade to carry visitors between town and station in horse carriages. The one-horse station bus was fondly remembered as a rattly old thing that had a peculiar smell of old straw and stuffiness.

Cromer Beach station was opened in 1887

At that time a grand scheme was put forward to sell off and develop parts of the Cromer Hall Estate in two great swathes; one on the west cliff and the other between the town and the new station. But when the Lord of the Manor, John Bond Cabbell, died, his widow Margaret was disinclined to see the scheme through and nothing came of it. It was another ten years before an extension to the line was opened, which had a loop down to Cromer Beach then onward to Sheringham. This gave connections via the new railway town of Melton Constable with the Midlands.

By the turn of the century the journey direct from Liverpool Street to Cromer had been reduced to 2 hours 55 minutes and a weekend return ticket cost as little as 10 shillings (50p). This naturally encouraged excursionists to visit Cromer (and Sheringham). Throughout the 1890s the growth of passenger traffic and increases in accommodation went hand in hand. The peak year for passenger arrivals at Cromer Beach station was 1907.

Royal patronage

Cromer was very keen to attact the patronage of rich and famous people. A particularly important visitor was the beautiful Empress Elizabeth of Austria, the estranged wife of Franz Joseph. This tragic lady broke free from her strange and unhappy life of court engagements in Europe seeking peace and sanctuary. Her staff failed to secure accommodation at Locker-Lampson's Newhaven Court and were unable to rent Cliff House from Sir Samuel Hoare. Arrangements were finally made for her to take an entire suite in the promenade annexe of Tucker's Hotel, much to the pleasure of proprietor Alex Jarvis. She came directly to Cromer by special train in June 1887 and stayed almost two months. She was terrified of being poisoned and was most particular in the preparation of her food, having her bread

Queen Alexandra is escorted to Cromer High station after staying with Lord Hillingdon in 1902

The club house of the Royal Cromer Golf Club in Happy Valley in the late 1890s: golf was an important part of Cromer's attraction

baked under supervision and a cow milked beneath her window. Despite her desire for solitude, the visitors could not contain themselves, staring and thronging around her whenever she appeared. Cromer's own Sergeant Lovick, officer in charge of the police station, was detailed to be her bodyguard.

The Prince of Wales was friendly with Lord Suffield of Gunton Hall who was instrumental in much of the development that went on. When a consortium laid out the golf course and erected the Links Hotel in 1895 they were sure to invite the Prince along to play and he became its patron. The club was styled the Royal Cromer Golf Club. The clubhouse was a pagoda-like corrugated iron shed which had formerly been a butcher's shop in Hamilton Road. The Prince also owned Tudor House in Cliff Avenue, where he entertained. Princess Stephanie (widow of the Empress Elizabeth's son) stayed there on the second of her visits to Cromer. In 1901 it was widely expected that the king would build a seaside residence at Cromer but this never materialised.

Growth in Poppyland

Without railways Cromer could not have grown to the extent that it did. But the descriptions of Cromer, north Norfolk and the east coast generally by Clement Scott in the 1880s and 1890s were another factor that gave an added boost to the fortunes of the town. In his sentimental writings the famous journalist and theatre critic dubbed the area 'Poppyland' and with that, conveyed romance and colour which was seized on by the promoters of Cromer. Within a short while 'Poppyland' had been adopted wholesale by souvenir retailers, hoteliers, railway companies and local authorities all eager to bring holidaymakers and excursionists

Westward development: the Grand Hotel (right) and the Marlborough (with cupola). Between them building in Cabbell Road are going up piecemeal.

to the area. One of Scott's poems, 'The Garden of Sleep', celebrating the lonely church tower on the cliff at Sidestrand, was set to music and became very popular. Before long 'Poppyland' was a household word and its virtues widely renowned. A full account of the Poppyland legend is given in another book in this series.

Once the Beach station had opened in 1887 a new spirit pervaded the town and growth and development proceeded apace. Until then Cromer had quaint little streets, primitive shops and other unconventional characteristics. Mrs Bond Cabbell, the Lady of the Manor, had discouraged building. But by 1890 the land speculators perceived that a revolution was going on. Mrs Bond Cabbell's son had come of age and he was keen on making money. No wonder developers cheered him heartily at public meetings. As a consequence, building was in progress in all directions. The first big sale of land from the Cromer Hall estate in 1890 was under the direction of Mr A. Baker, an auctioneer from London who specialised in selling seaside land to speculators. Cromer was patently ripe for investment and there was a larger than expected attendance. Bidding was keen and land fetched very high prices indeed. Some 72 plots in Station Road, Bernard Road, Macdonald Road and Alfred Road were sold. Meanwhile, the Grand Hotel was being built on a nearby site, adjacent to the Marrams west of the town. The following year 73 more plots were sold from Prince of Wales Road and Station Road. The two sales raised over £14,000 and opened up the west of the town for building development, which has mainly been in the form of boarding houses and apartments and hotels.

George Skipper, the Norwich architect who designed the attractive art nouveau arcade there, also obtained several valuable commissions to design hotels and residences at Cromer in this boom time. The Grand Hotel previously mentioned was his design (alas damaged by fire in 1969 and demolished in 1971). It was boldly ornamented with white detailing set against red brick and with high French roofs.

◀ *'The red brick badge of modern seaside prosperity': Norwich Road in 1895*

He also designed the Metropole Hotel (1893) between Tucker Street and the sea (which never recovered after its wartime occupation and was replaced by de Vere Court in 1985). The Hotel de Paris, which still survives and so sets the style of the skyline, with its commanding position overlooking the pier, is also Skipper's but this time an adaptation and extension of the original building (1894). There were several commissions for houses including the pair which guard the entrance to Cliff Avenue from Norwich Road.

Meanwhile, the streets in the town were changing too in the last quarter of the nineteenth century. It seems hard to imagine that until this time much of the land to the south of Church Street was still undeveloped, with gardens and fields coming right to the roadside. The 1890s saw large houses and terraces sprouting up Norwich Road, Overstrand Road and Cliff Avenue and infilling continued right through the twentieth century. It was not until the 1980s that the old bowling green on the corner of Overstrand Road went for housing.

The changing character of the place was not to everybody's taste, and modern critics of Cromer architecture will sympathise with this journalist, although Cromer has undoubtedly changed its appeal since 1901.

> Cromer, when you get into it, wears the red brick badge of modern seaside prosperity. Not only on the (West) Cliff and on the surrounding hillsides, but

throughout the town, you come upon the well-meant mistakes of modern architecture. The shops cater for the well-lined purses - that you understand at a glance. The hotels, the Paris, the Grand, the Metropole would probably scorn the family of modest means. The brand new whiteness and freshness of pier and pavilion bear witness to recent expenditure. Altogether the evidence of Cromer's wealth and good fortune is almost aggressive.

An unusual view of Cromer c.1880 from the window of Hagley House looking east. Mr Sandford's garden is now occupied by the sorting office, Jarrolds and HSBC bank.

The parish church after the restoration of the tower in 1885. The chancel was rebuilt in 1889 and part of the churchyard was taken for road widening.

The huge and magnificent church, in Perpendicular style, has the tallest tower of any in Norfolk. But in the seventeenth and eighteenth centuries it had become too much for the local congregation to maintain and the fabric began to decay. The chancel was practically in ruins and Rev Thomas Gill took gunpowder to it in 1681, leaving only parts of the walls standing. By 1767 the roof of the nave and aisles had fallen in and the rest was in such poor shape that it was estimated that it would cost £1,000 to repair. To raise at least some of the money the lead was sold, as were four of the bells, which reputedly went to St Mary le Bow (the famous Bow Bells of Cockney London), By the mid-nineteenth century the church was in a very sorry state with no chancel, bricked up windows, flints missing from the tower and a tiled roof. Until 1863 the tower showed a single-handed clock but in that year the present one was endowed by wealthy local residents. This was accompanied by extensive renovations to the nave and aisles. In 1885 began the restoration of the tower, and then the rebuilding of the chancel on the old foundations. By 1889 the church was restored to full glory thanks to generous local benfactors.

Urban growth

In 1884 a Local Board was established to run various local government functions and one of its most important acts was to negotiate a lease on the foreshore with the Lords of the Manors, Lord Suffield and Benjamin Bond-Cabbell. This gave them power to regulate the use of the beach and control the numerous itinerants such as minstrels, hawkers and swingboat and stall operators. The Mace Brothers' camera obscura (a darkened wooden cubicle with a table, onto which the image of scenes outside was projected) was banned and Mr Bower was given notice to quit his refreshment tent, which had served at the bottom of the Gangway for 17 years.

In 1894 the Local Board was replaced by the Cromer Urban District Council with its offices in Pump House (now Lloyds TSB) between Chapel Street and West Street. The local authorities were aware of the importance for the town's image of the correct arrangements being made for public bathing. Respectability would dictate that during bathing, men and women should be segregated either in space or in time and by-laws forbade so-called mixed bathing. Indignant articles in the *Cromer and North Walsham Post* pilloried some visitors for violations of common decency, such as whole families using the same bathing machine, or even gentlemen hiring a boat to row parallel with the shore until the female bathing ground was reached and then stripping off and diving in naked. In Council meetings some thought the wearing of scanty bathing drawers for swimming quite indecent, others just laughed and thought the whole matter petty.

The beach in August 1888 before the introduction of regulations which controlled commercial use of the foreshore. On the extreme left is Herbert Mace's camera obscura in an octagonal hut. Other attractions include a Romany caravan (?fortune teller), swing boats, coconut shy, retail stalls, bathing machines and costumes for hire; fishermen are taking passengers in the boats.

The by-laws provided clear places and times for men and women to use the bathing grounds but the politicians were quite aware of the counter arguments. How absurd it was that Papa must loll in the surf half a mile distant from his beloved wife and tender young daughters, who could well need his strong arm in the buffeting waves and benefit from his tuition in the art of swimming. They were equally aware of course that foreign resorts had no such restrictions and that Cromer was in competition with them. The minutes of the Council meetings are surprisingly silent on the debates that must have ensued but in April 1898 new by-laws allowed mixed bathing, though restricted to certain parts of the beach, at certain times of day. The rules were further relaxed in 1907, still providing of course that the gentlemen wore a suitable costume from neck to knee. So far as we know this official acceptance of the widespread change in moral attitude predates any other resort in Britain. Many places which traditionally catered for working class visitors still maintained strict segregation into the 1920s. Cromer, despite its classy aspirations, or perhaps because of them, was progressive.

In step with the great changes brought about by development, came the necessary improvements in public amenities and utilities. The introduction of electric light was a controversial matter but eventually in 1903 a steam driven generator was built in Central Road and operated by a private company, Messers Edmondsons. The water works was a private company formed in 1875, with a well and borehole sunk on the Norwich Road. When this supply became inadequate for the growing town and surrounding villages a larger one was built at Metton, with a deep boring into the chalk. This was acquired by the Urban District Council, and included a reservoir at Roman Camp.

The East Beach in 1885

All those new beds provided a lot of linen for the Cromer Steam Laundry Company in Cross Street

Fishermen's cottages off Surrey Street in the 1960s, now demolished

FREE SCHOOL
FOUNDED BY
S^{IR} BARTHOLOMEW READ K^{NT}
A.D.1505
NATIVE OF CROMER, LORD MAYOR OF LONDON
BUILT AND ENDOWED BY THE
GOLDSMITHS COMPANY
OF LONDON
A.D.1821.

Schools

The Free School

Cromer was exceedingly lucky to have a proper school from a very early time. The Goldsmiths' or Free School was founded in 1505 by the will of Sir Bartholomew Reed (Rede) a goldsmith and alderman in London 'to teach gentlemen's sons and good men's children and especially poor men's children, of the said town and the country there abouts'. Reed vested lands and property in the Goldsmiths' Company, the income from which was to provide a salary of £10 a year for the master who was to be a priest and a graduate, preferably one who had been through Eton or Winchester. The Goldsmiths' lands were situated between the East Cliff and Overstrand Road. We can't be sure but things must have continued for centuries much as they were in Reed's day until in 1821 the Goldsmiths' Company provided for a new school building, which is still there, constructed of neat pebbles and yellow brick and which has also served as a doctor's surgery. Simeon Simons was for many years the master of the school and up to 100 boys between the ages of six and 14 received instruction in the tiny building. If their parents were poor, the schooling was free. By 1886 the changes in Cromer were rendering the school insufficient and out of touch with modern ideas of efficiency. 'The provision for education which were ample for the fishing village of 50 years ago will soon become obsolete,' said a report. As Cromer had undergone many changes in the late nineteenth century and was comparatively wealthy, the Company reconsidered its obligation to provide free education in the town. With the coming of the Board School in 1896 the Free School was closed down and Reed's endowment was converted to an exhibition (annual award) to assist local scholars in higher education.

The Girls' School

In the middle of the nineteenth century, education for infants was undertaken by Rev W. Sharpe and later by Rev Frederick Fitch and his daughters. The school was in Church Street on the site of the present Parish Hall but not in that building. The first qualified teacher came in 1872 and she and her two successors laboured with inadequate resources to teach the infants and older girls of the district. In summer the girls were often absent in order to take up seasonal work, which in the booming resort was in the hotel and catering trades. They frequently suffered from outbreaks of infectious diseases (such as scarlet fever, typhoid, tuberculosis and diphtheria) which robbed them of numbers when the children were sick or even died, or their parents kept them away for fear of infection. In 1895 the autocratic Dr Fenner ordered the closure of the school, probably due to an infection. The school was to close permanently when in 1896 the School Board opened its new premises in Cross Street.

Children of school age seen in Garden Street about the 1870s

The site of the former Board School has been thoughtfully and sensibly converted into housing. It is now known as Norman Trollor Court, maintaining the tradition of naming streets after respected citizens who contributed much to the town.

Boys and their teacher at the newly opened Board School in 1896. Note the variety of 'best' clothes for the photographer, including fishermen's ganseys and Norfolk jackets.

The Board School

In 1895 education in the town was organised under the Cromer School Board, although until the new school was ready the old premises continued to be used. They erected the new school – amid a public outcry denouncing lack of financial controls – in 1896. It was in fact three schools on a single site, each with its entrance, head teacher and classrooms. The High School on the Norwich Road was fully opened in 1949, whilst the Junior Mixed School continued in the old premises and with the incumbent headmistress continuing in post. Although in its day it was considered to be a model school, ideas changed and it moved into new buildings on the Norwich Road in 1994.

Station Road, Suffield Park, still developing in 1914. On the left is the Suffield Park Hotel, which was then large enough to accommodate fifty guests and was conveniently situated opposite Cromer High station. In the background the massive Royal Links Hotel dominates the skyline of the Lighthouse Hills.

Twentieth-century growth

The termination of the railway line from Norwich at the High Station and the development of Suffield Park go hand in hand. The land required for both was part of the parish of Overstrand and was largely in the hands of Lord Suffield, who was well disposed to development. Swathes of land were auctioned off in small lots with stipulations about the nature of the properties to be built there. When development started a great many houses went up with little regard to the sanitary consequences. The district had no sewer and all the houses had their own cesspools. These were in close proximity to wells as there was no public water supply either. All the roads were private and none of them was made up. Public health was at dire risk and application was made to tunnel under the Lighthouse Hills in order to take sewerage out into the sea but Cromer objected that it would be washed back onto the beaches and would ruin the bathing. The upshot was that the Urban District Council annexed Suffield Park to Cromer and this new area of development was connected to Cromer's long sewer outfall. Development of Suffield Park was at first piecemeal but gradually the entire area was covered with houses and villas and the roads were eventually brought up to a standard similar to the rest of the town.

The late twentieth century saw continued growth in the rest of Cromer, especially of housing estates, and while the holiday industry saw a great change, with the closure of one hotel after another, the area increasingly attracted people wishing to retire to the town. Clement Scott had previously lamented that his beloved Poppyland had become Bungalow Land. If only he could see it now! In the last decade of the 20th century the added pressures of Caravan Land continued to grow and venerable Edwardian hotels have been replaced with flats or converted for residential or holiday use. Cromer became the resort it did because of what it inherited: character. It was recognised that if Cromer was to continue to attract a holiday trade it would do well to preserve and make

Two views of Church Street: above, an early engraving hinting at the poor condition of the houses before wealthy visitors brought the town up-market a bit! Below, a photograph taken from almost the same viewpoint in 1964, shortly before the widening of 'The Narrows'.

The pleasant tumble of buildings down the cliff face at Cromer is best seen in early morning light, before the sun moves around to put the scene into shade.

good use of the best of that inheritance.

This was at the back of all proposals as a 'Regeneration Plan' was put forward early in the new century. All layers of local governnment, together with many other interested persons and groups, met over an extended period to consider a new range of developments made possible by European funding allocated to Cromer and Suffield Park. The promise of the greatest co-ordinated spend on infrastructure since the heyday of the late Victorian and Edwardian building boom required much thought and effort, and a considerable balancing act. Some were of the opinion that nothing should be altered, others were of the opinion that coming to Cromer was a less than desirable journey back in time.

The least controversial process was perhaps that of simply ensuring that the

The addition of two shops at the promenade end of the pier and the H.F.Bailey lifeboat compass and the 'rescue lines' were part of the 'Regeneration' scheme.

The Rocket House on the left, the extension to the pier pavilion and the rebuilt lifeboat house are relatively modern additions to the pleasing mix of buildings on the seafront.

several buildings that were eyesores in the town were tackled and this process was carried out largely by carrot and occasionally by stick. The net result was that many other property owners gained confidence and also took the opportunity to improve their buildings. The requirement for the improvement of facilities on the pier was addressed through a range of new developments and the pier forecourt underwent a transformation, with a change of style and the inclusion of the lifeboat compass and its 'rescue lines'.

Carnival, the COAST arts festival and the early season Crab and Lobster Festival featured in our picture are amongst the seasonal offerings enjoyed by townsfolk and visitors.

The happy coincidence of a substantial bequest to enable a lifeboat museum to be built, together with the enterprise of the District Council and European funding enabled the somewhat utilitarian Rocket House on the east promenade to be replaced by a distinctive new building, designed around the conservation and display requirements for the *H.F.Bailey* lifeboat. The earlier building was a 1950s replacement for the café which had stood on the site until it had received a direct hit from an enemy bomb in 1940. There was concern over the concept of a new building on the seafront but the general realisation that the mix of buildings represented over 200 years of construction, with a pleasant variety rather than a co-ordinated unity, meant a 21st century Rocket House went ahead. The considerable footfall that both the Henry Blogg Lifeboat Museum and the Rocket House Café attract suggests the bold decision was correct.

The three purpose-built hospitals. The 1883 hospital in Louden Road, enlarged in 1904; the 1932 building in Mill Road; the new building on the same site in 2012

The search for the site for a new hospital for the town occupied much time over a 15 year period. The extremely generous bequest of some £11.4 million by Mrs Sagle Bernstein caused consternation and heartache but eventually it was confirmed that it could be spent on bricks and mortar. The changing requirements and abilities of modern health care have led to the loss of overnight beds but the new building, with a Minor Injuries Unit and a range of leading edge facilities, is a great credit to a generous donor, as was the previous hospital to Lady Battersea and her fellow fund raisers.

And so we conclude this edition - other Poppyland Publishing titles and DVDs will enable the interested reader to dig much deeper into the town's story.

Index